Sparks of Words

Sparks of Words

Grish Davtian

RESOURCE *Publications* • Eugene, Oregon

SPARKS OF WORDS

Resource Publications
An Imprint of Wipf and Stock Publishers
199 W. 8th Ave., Suite 3
Eugene, OR 97401

www.wipfandstock.com

PAPERBACK ISBN: 978-1-7252-6532-5
HARDCOVER ISBN: 978-1-7252-6522-6
EBOOK ISBN: 978-1-7252-6523-3

Manufactured in the U.S.A. 06/23/20

Contents

The cricket screeches and scoffs,
The cricket squeaks and lectures,
As if inquires in the depth of the night
The deep secrets of life.

Glendale CA 20040324

Old Song of Guitar

The radio is broadcasting an old tune
The tune seems to be weeping.

When was it . . . I used to love you,
I remember you by that tune.

Now whenever it resounds
All my memories scramble.

Glendale CA 20040324

Prayer

Cherish me like the creator,
Dispel my sadness;
I have fallen into a deadlock,
Into interminable torments.

My glowing hopes have
Departed with my dreams;
Without leaving any rustle,
Any rosy hue.

Now it is black and the dark
Covering my esteemed wishes;
The wings of my flight are broken
On the cliffs of calamity.

My white-breasted swallow
Came across with an evil arrow;
The ignoble fraudulent hand
Set up a snare and intrigue.

Cherish me and console me,
Put an end to this torture;
Grant hope to my heart, and illuminate,
Brighten up my dark days.

Break the conspiracy,
Break the insidious hand ten folds;
Raise the wounded swallow of my hopes
Into the heights of the blue.

So that I may achieve my aims,
Approach my creator.
Lights and hopes . . . my heart and soul
May gather strength in happiness.

Glendale CA 20040324

Days On

See, the sun shines,
The moon winks,
The stars twinkle brightly
In the distances of the sky;
The long rows of the days
That have spun the length of years,
Stretch from childhood
And connect with today.

Yet in the twist of the thread,
In the folds of the years,
What a kind of life,
Made into balls of thread, twists, and folds,
And memories have bunched together.

Accumulated a sense of loss,
Sweet and burning,
With a heart beating intimacy,
And kin warmth,
With clear love and devotion,
Fervor and contribution,
Creative labor,
Campaign and victory,
A hailing here,
A face there,
Sweet glance yonder,
Touches your heart and soul,
Burns with yearning . . .

The heart feels squeezed, gasping,
With memories of years,
Full of the plenty of familiar expanses,
And the warmth of embraces.

The roads and days
Woven together in a colorful rosette
Are stretched in the blue,
From horizon to horizon,
From the distance of today
The deep nostalgia resounds
In the long and uninterrupted interval,
From home to heart,
Sweetened with feelings
With a rainbow of love.

With olden devotions,
And energetic reflections,
With the merits of years,
Brimful benefices,
A meaningful life
By which the worthy forehead is decorated
With gleaming brightness,
By which the heart beats
Under the chest
With harmonic throbbing hymn.

The old eagle with hang wings,
But still hovering in the high,
In his eyes is a saintly image
Of unreturnable past,
In his eyes is a treasured promise,
In his eyes is an old spark.

And the sun blinks,
And the moon blinks.

Glendale CA 20040330

Of Feeling, of Love, of Devotion, of Longing and of Memory

O, my soft songs of bygone days,
I am not longing for you at all,
I am longing for the feelings
By which I sang you.

I sang my colorful love,
My true devotion;
I am longing for that love,
I am longing for her love,
And my innocent dedication.

And I turn these pages,—
Emotional soft songs
Dripping from their words and lines
All longings and memories of past.

Glendale CA 20040330

Of Winter

She wants to put her arms around me . . .
So, she says it is cold,
Steam rises from her lips;
I reject her, I do not care,
The moment is so cruel,
I am mournful with memories.

She, who is a whitish, beautiful girl,
Envies, and burst on to me,
Although she embraces me,
But only like a touch,
And withdraws proudly in time.

Her touch is smooth and fragile
Like the snow,
Whitish and soft girlish,
The night of her eyes is infinite,
Where I simply get lost.

My heart feels grave . . . in the cold of winter
I fling myself . . . and nearly clasp her . . .
But she melts away like the rime of night,
Leaving her wet kiss on my lips.

I know, she melted from the grief of my rejection,
She is just a whitish, beautiful girl;
Oh, I cannot put her out of my mind,
Just as a fleeting free love.

Glendale CA 20040405

Spring Is a Girl

Penetrated my heart with flowers of the garden,
She is a girl with rosy cheeks,
Spring is her name, she scents of maturity
With an open collar shirt on herself.

The hot light of her bosom pricks my eyes,
Her lips are ripe as peaches;
Her hearty love blossoms with roses,
She tells me to pick them.

So juicy . . . I relish it like a bee.
She tells me not to, as it is lethal.
I do not know whether it is death, poison, or a feast,
I feel giddy, as merry go round.

Her name is spring, she is all over my chest,
She scents like rose petals;
I feel breathless, she has thorns on her hands,
And sometimes stings severely.

But suddenly she becomes a string of beads,
Hanging from my neck, shining,
She turns all my anxieties into a deep sigh,
Throws it to the breeze and laughs.

She whispers softly to my ear and tells me,
Tells me tales of spring;
A mature girl she is with rosy cheeks,
Wearing a cheap floral shirt.

Glendale CA 20040406

Spring

You arrive in her fresh footsteps,
Through the twirling and flowing path,
From where she has passed with light steps,
But has sunk into my heart
As a warm and bright ray,
That flows with my blood,
With feeling and harmony,
Whirl-pooling, deepening,
Deepening.
And from the depths of my heart
Sprouts like a lit blossom,
With the good tidings of the waking nature,
As a blue flower
Which is a bright shred of a dream,
A heartening promise
Lingering under the sun,
Breathing with her scent,
Caressing my temples,
Smearing her warmth on my lips
With a yearning of my kisses.

You arrive with her finicky gait,
Twisting her thin waist,
Avoiding my embrace,
Like the cloud, which clasps to the moon
But slips from the crescent,
And piles up like the solemn dreams of my frown.

You arrive through those remote roads
From where my dreams pass
With irretrievable memories,
Spinning the secret story of my life
With dramatic fascination;
Through the pastures of my desires,
Where my needs graze
Like innocent lambs.

My desires exult like butterflies,
On whose wings you arrive.
You arrive with her thrill
And enter my heart.

I worship your flowering,
The petals of which
She sprinkled on my chest
As compassion and happiness.
I worship your narcissi
With gold cups
Full of dew, by which
The nightingales of my wishes got drunk,
Warbling ode to her.
I worship your violets,
Your white jasmines,
By which you are ornamented
And thus, resembling her,
Become worthy of my adoration.

With the peace of the mornings
Inseminate my desires,
So that in my supplication
I may feel the taste of her kisses;
Admire her beauty
With the assurance of my loyalty
And feel my dedication
With the warmth of my love,
By which you arrive with a renewed life,
You arrive unchanged as a continuation,
And grant taste and scent,
As of lasting copiousness,
As meaningful returns of solemn departures.

You arrive,
Enter my heart,
And flourish.

Glendale CA 20041017

Ripeness

This year
Autumn has exploded in blond,
It has exploded in red;
Autumn has smeared
A puff of cloud
On my hair and beard,
Autumn has sprinkled
A pinch of salt
To sweeten my life.

Your cheeks have turned red
Like the dawns and
Like the sunsets;
Your cheeks have turned red.
But the twist
By which you twirl your waist
Is in the ring of my arms . . .
In the ring of my arms . . .

A warmth flashes through my palms,
I desire to feel your touch
From which I shivered that night . . .
I shivered . . .

There is warmth in my palms now,
There is warmth in my temples now,
My heart is pounding
In your warm bosom.

My devotion is colorful in blond,
Your devotion is sparkling in red;
Autumn has flared up in ripeness . . .
In ripeness . . .

Glendale CA 20041017

Her Name Is Autumn

A blond lass is waiting on my path,
With humid lips, barefoot,
Her braided hair in the breeze, topless, thin,
I like her, her name is Autumn.

I call her, and she holds me in her arms,
Fills the pits of my path with fallen leaves,
Wets my lips with the rain,
Whispers to my ear, that her name is Autumn.

I want to take her home as my bride,
To care for me and to love me,
To cuddle me at night in her warm bosom,
To tell me she loves me,
To tell me that her name is Autumn.

Blond Autumn . . . blond Autumn . . .
Oh, my colorful memories . . .
Fallen and scattered in my heart
Like roses and thorns . . .
I want her every day and night . . .
And cannot forget that her name is Autumn . . .

Glendale CA 20041018

Golden Autumn

I never loved you,
Yet I eulogized you often,
Golden Autumn
Of nature
And my life;
Yet, you always
Scattered in my pathway
Your withered leaves,
And your abundant fruits,
Ripe and delicious.

If I never had
The blossoming of the spring
With its torrent of warmth;
The original instinct, holy and creative,
To love and to possess;
If I never had the heat of the summer,
And the charge which boils my blood;
If I never had . . .
I would have worshipped your gold,
The harvest of all those experiences
I stored day by day in the tower of my years,
Becoming full and conscious and thoughtful.

If I never had
The stipulate conception of super pursuits
Of the swift world,
Exploding, waning, reviving, crumbling,
Conquering
Every moment;
If I never had
The inherited flame of my earthly gene,
From superstring atom
Of the great chaos,

Creator and destroyer;
If I never had . . .
Oh, then,
I would never have been that bee
Who lived
With the fiery passion to possess the flowers;
That dew
To clasp to the petals of roses with coolness;
That breeze that combs the skulls of the peaks . . .
I would never have been,
I would never have been what I am.

Golden autumn,
Golden autumn,
I never loved you;
Although I mold your gold,
Although I dedicate my songs
To the sprouting and blossoming of spring,
To the assured swooping maturity,
Filled with the warmth of summer
With the strength of pleasured bequeathal.

And now,
In the golden stall of your abundance,
Anointed with the ripeness of the sun,
And violet rays of distant,
From whence to wherever
Ascending with decent dignity,
With intentional aim,
And with irreproachable and virile dissatisfaction,
Golden autumn,
Let me not remain indebted to you.

Glendale CA 20041223

Violet Petals

She is a verdurous flower with violet petals,
She is a tender girl, scenting like a violet,
On her honeyed lips are words of love,
And in her honey-colored eyes are violet dreams.

She has arrived with longings of distant lands,
And has perched in the warm depths of my heart,
She is showering on me petals of violet,
Narrating for me stories of heart and love.

There has been a day rising with the sun of youth,
And a happy youngster wandering in the garden,
Who used to catch butterflies and was fascinated with colors,
But kept his secrets of what he felt.

He has kept in his memories the glitter of her eyes,
By which he was struck and singed . . .
She is now flitting about in his front,
But he is unable to catch her with his trembling fingers.

I am trembling with the shiver of admiration and love,
I am bristling up by the love of my youth days . . .
She is a tender girl, scenting like a flower,
She is showering on me petals of violet.

Glendale CA 20041223

Broken Promise

They all promised to my loving heart . . .

The sun promised to rise
And paint the day with light . . .

The moon promised to renew always
And shave the chin of the night
With the sharp edge of the crescent . . .

The stars promised to glitter
And spray dews to the fiery flowers,
To wet the tows of the breeze
When it touches the petals . . .

You promised my loving heart . . .

Your eyes promised your love;
Your lips promised to extinguish
My flames with kisses.

And although the sun rises
And paints the day with light;
The moon renews and slides
With the light-and-dark patterns;
The stars glitter proudly,
Dews fall on the petals of roses
Wetting the lips of the breeze . . .

Yet all your given promises remain
As of passing melody of words only . . .

My desire seeks you with a rustle
But does not reach to your guilty kisses.

Glendale CA 20041223

With Secrecy

The sunset of autumn wrings
Tears of the clouds on my pale face
with scent;
What past sins am I expiating
That gives me such a heartbeat?

It is a shred of a secret story:
That you looked for the first time,
That I stayed indifferent witness,
And your glance broke away reluctantly.

A play of light and shadow:
That I did not realize you desired me . . .
An illusion of a mad dreamer
Which is still clear as an innocent imagination.

A voice is rising from the depth of my longing
Whining in my solitude;
What unrepented sin am I expiating
Secretly kept in my heart.

Glendale CA 20041228

Everlasting Tale

In the warm days of this late summer
My heart is filled
With cool desires of an early spring,
So that you would come to me
With immaculate love of youth,
As was the dew on the petals of a flower, _
So, with that ancient feeling,
Which was new to me,
Which was love,
Or was not,
Perhaps it truly was love,
Which I had newly found in my life,—
To hold your hand
And pull you close to me,
Your breasts would bump to my proud chest,
I would look into the depth of your eyes,
As if into the clear lake of the mirror,
Where always, always
I used to feel warmer,
I used to melt you more,
You used to become mine submissively,
With purified nakedness,
With cleanness of love . . .

In these warm days of late summer
My cool desires of this sparkling spring
Are heaving abundantly,
I possess you with earned devotion,
Which has cultivated the sweat
Of diligence of my faithfulness . . .

You are fresh and delicate,
Budding,
And it suffices me to touch you,
With the sure strength of holy creation,
You bloom abruptly with colorful flowers
To fill my spring and my summer
With the glory of beauty and delight
That the suns never denied me
In the dispersions of diasporas,
But endowed me with your kisses,
And your entire caresses . . .

Do hover in my heart
Which is, perhaps, the greater part of this world
With the clear intensity of blue sky;
No rose has ever withered there,
But has sprouted with noble scent,
Even for a while,
Until you have given it a new start,
And the start is always like a complete spring . . .

The mornings are colorful and fresh,
Fly with me
With the flight of my interrupted dream,
The shred of which is still on my eyelids
And the blue tale of my world
Has no ending . . .

In the warm days of this late summer
My cool desires of an early spring
Carry the vessel loaded with flowers
To the remoteness of the blue sea of my shoreless heart,
Where you reign imperiously
Embracing the oars of love and hope,
Where you have dipped yourself in the clear craving,
Reaching to the depths of my delights too,
Which have no ending
Like the tales of my emotions.

This fine tale of my deep wishes
Sweetened with the aroma of summer and spring
Still tastes on my tongue
With the oozing sweetness of your kisses
And have no ending.

Glendale CA 20050108

Peacefully

The peace you bring me
Is like the ripple-sway of the field,
Which snatches me out of exhausting anxieties,
Takes me to the seclusion of my soft wishes,
Close to my heart,
Like my desire . . .
That you embrace me with pure happiness
Endow me the honey and wine of love
With the total plush taste of your lips . . .

Hug me strongly
So, my anxieties will be strangled in the loop of your arms;
Cover my neck with myriad kisses,
Press your palms to my burning temples
And spread your bosom on my chest . . .

That which is ripening with devotion
Let last long as the chime,
Which shudders me causing gooseflesh,
Which has a mad hop of teens,
Crashes with the dispersion of a wave,
And calms down with ebbing,
Panting with a deep breath,
Exhausting tiredness . . .

Bring peace to my struggling soul,
To enjoy the victory of love,
To acquire the instinct of belonging,
And cherish you with content in my realm.

Now with heartfelt desires
I am yielding to your carrying sways;
With a sacred loyalty of a unique wish
I am taking you in my arms,
Flying and taking you
Beyond the arch of the rainbow
Woven in seven colors,
To the colorful world of love . . .

Breathe my breath,
So that I may inhale you with insemination,
To bloom lilies in the kernel of your heart,
And open the blue secret of life;
With reconciled peace
Reward you with my tranquility
In the azure depth of the horizon,
Which you regaled me serenely . . .

The peace that you present me
Is like the calm wave of the field,
Like the calm wave . . .

Glendale CA 20051107

The First Sin

With dreams of violet hue
And with panting of wistful memories
I remember
That awesome mystery night of the old, decrepit village . . .

The golden sun shrouded its rays
In the blushing west,
The dark throng of shredded shadows
Arrived without any melody . . .
The thin black veil
With flights of delicate dreams
Censed sleep
From the eaves of steep roofs.
In the expanding shroud of the pale moonlight
The weary village fell asleep with blue thoughts.

Sacred promises in our hearts
We walked through the waves of newly plowed fields
To the ruined cathedral,
To kiss the stone-crosses there.

The shadows stretched out along our way
Like fire worshiping majestic priests.

We knelt in the courtyard of the stone-crosses
To offer our sacred prayers,
Sacred and bright prayers,
Dedicated to each other,
While holding our secret love as an altar
In the innocence of our hearts.

The elusive phantoms of heavenly, vain saints
Flocked around us
Scared of our divine prayers.
While the spirits soared gently above us
We concluded our prayers and vows,
And kissed the stone-crosses in the courtyard.

But there was one stone-cross standing vehemently tall,
Holding high its proud and smooth forehead,
That we could not kiss.
You implored, and I helped you up on my shoulders,
You embraced and kissed the stone-cross,
Yet, I remained there below
Deprived of the blessing of the unattainable kiss
Of that stone-cross.

Then you slid down . . . On our way back
When we sat by the spring,
I plucked the kiss of that cold stone-cross from your warm lips.

I wish . . . I wish I had lost my faith in the old ruined cathedral,
So that with the thoughts of that stone-cross
I would not contaminate our pure emotions and feelings . . .

Glendale CA 20060309

Heart to Heart

When I am gone
And you desire
The warmth of my love,
Go to the garden on a sunny day
As a visitor to the flowers
That I have sowed wholeheartedly
On the pages of my emotions;
The fresh blossoms of my songs will give
The scent of love
To your desires.

Even if far away
I will be close to you in love,
In the blue horizon,
In the ether.

There was an old, faraway street
We walked through it so often,
I am keeping an insignificant memory of it,
So close to my heart,
Though slightly dusty,
Yet ornamented
With your sweet glances.

It was a fortune, or was not,
But it was a life
Full of charms and lovability,
That will last even differently
If cut short by old age.

It has been achieved by maturity,
And is not measured by time.

A mixture of light and dark,
With the capacity of the horizon,
As the capacity of your emotions,
Of my emotions scented with roses.

Open the pages of my love
With warmth and softness,
Hold tight to your bosom,
Like I embraced you,
Whisper my words,
The story of our love,
That weaved the happiness of our life
In numerous colors of beauty
And chiming in our hearts.

It was a life, a song,
A desirable devotion.

Glendale CA 20061229

Moon-Bark

A dream is oozing from the censer of the moon,
A blue delusion;
Foam is chewing moss in the lagoon,
Lukewarm and humid.

In the golden ray of the moon, a shadow stirred,
A sleepwalker bastard;
The breeze scattered from the folds of the dark
Gravel and sand.

The sky is turned over the earth,
Seizing sparks;
Sparkling stars gleaming faraway,
My dazzling wishes.

I wish to bend over your bosom with love,
Let the flash break out;
In our hearts, in the whole universe
Ferment will erupt.

And the azure horizon fluctuates,
Falls into slumber;
Is it a dream of a sleepwalker, or a nightmare?
Howls in the dark.

It's jaws against the silver of the moon
The dog barks;
My ardent ardor, your Milky Way bosom,
Your panting, the rustle.

Glendale CA 20061229

Your cheeks are colorful like the apple,
Your lips are juicy like the apricot,
As an arch of the rainbow in the sky of love,
You are melting in my embrace like a snowflake.

Glendale CA 20070103

Faithfulness

The sea moans in the tranquility of the azure night,
Heaping its fluid back in the lights of the shore;
The pure flames wriggle and break like crystal,
Floating with the whisper of playful numerous waves.

With an infinite meaning, the sea moans from depths,
That has underlined a gold-color mysticism in my life;
The stars, which are born from my eyes and wishes,
Are scattered in the blue atmosphere,
As sparks in my heart.

So many breezes caressed the wide sea of my bold forehead,
Caressed the longing of my eyes, with the illusions of afar;
With the shreds of my fiery thoughts, which are these whole clouds,
Sacrificed the virginity of the horizon imperturbably.

They are silent now. And I am silent, too, with the total of my words,
I have kneaded them with the taste and bloom of life and corn;
My wishes are forming up, the sea is moaning fathomlessly,
Pounding the shores of the past and of the present.

Love is exceptional. And the flames burn the darkness
At the littoral of the sea and land as sacrifice and devotion;
As a fantasy, as desire flashing to the close,
On life, on fortune as giggle and vow.

As if I do not exist. But my wishes do exist and will remain so,
They will become immortal like light, in the distance of my sight,
In the colossal mixture of earth and water, storm and fire,
By which my lips smile, by which my heart is faithful.

Glendale CA 20070103

Multilonging

I wandered excessively,
Stayed here and there protracted,
Made friends and became settled,
Yet suddenly roved about again.

Wherever I stayed I loved wholeheartedly,
And was loved by so many too;
But, what happened, did a breeze blow abruptly
And separated me from my loved ones?

Yet by leaving and going away
I took my loves with me in my heart;
I took with me their loves, memories, and affections,
Those have become my deep longings.

And now, wherever I may be,
Around me and in my bosom are my loved ones,
But in my heart is my longing of those
Who are far away, who are not in my arms.

Glendale CA 20070108

Dream-Flight

What a nice dream it was;
As if I was in our court . . .
Then I was riding a white horse . . .
Was it a horse . . . Was it you?
I was caressing you . . .
Perhaps it was a horse, and I was riding.

I was galloping fast like lightening,
I was flying in the clouds . . .
All neighbors were looking at me,
They were saying
"Look at him, he is the white horseman
Flying like the lightening". . .
They were gossiping:
"Look, he is the stupid guy in love
Who flies in his dreams". . .

As if it were our vineyard,
I was eating off the vine trees,
The grapes were ripe and sweet . . .
Or were your lips
I was kissing . . .
Ripe they were . . . sweet they were . . .

My father and brother were watering the vineyard . . .
As if I was falling from the vine trees . . .
But you were reaching down and catching me,
You were touching me with desire . . .
We were embracing . . .
We embraced . . .
We were flying
We were so light . . .
I was carrying you away . . .

It was a flight . . .
It was a quiver . . .
You were vibrating . . .
You were my vibration . . .

Glendale CA 20070108

Dream Glow

It was a dream . . .
It was blue, it was azure . . .
As if I was in my room . . .
I was wondering why the door was not there!
The closet was there,
And my big mirror was there
With its semicircular header.

It was a blue evening of warm summer . . .
The sun had swung towards West,
Reflecting in the mirror . . .
I was standing in the reflection
And caressing the sunrays . . .
Perhaps I was caressing your hips.

I just pushed myself up . . .
And I was flying up the sunrays . . .
I was curling around your hips . . .
As if it was sunrays . . .
As if it was you . . .
I was just pushing myself up . . .
Like I was flying . . .
As if I was embracing you . . .
Curling around you . . .
As if getting absorbed deeper . . .

It was blue, it was azure . . .
It was a blue evening of warm summer . . .
I was in my room . . .
There were my books . . . there were you . . .
At my desk, I was writing my poems,
Dedicating to you . . .

You were glowing . . .
I was writing on the glow . . .
I was so light,
I was flying . . .

My mother was calling me
To have my tea . . .

Glendale CA 20070108

Wet Dream

You came into my dream
With your same charm
And magic,
As if you were embracing me in the heavens . . .
You were kissing me with flirtations . . .
It seemed as if you were moving away . . .
Yet it seemed as if I was catching you . . .
Then the same play was repeating,
I was catching you and kissing you . . .
You were laughing . . .
I was envying you . . .

And then again you were running away . . .
Your pink skirt was waving . . .
Your full hips were vibrating . . .
As if my hands had embraced your hips,
And were burning,
And were caressing . . .
Close to my ear was the whisper of your breath . . .
I was feeling your warmth . . .

Then it seemed we were going away . . .
Then as if we entered from a door,
But there was no room, nothing behind the door,
So, we jumped,
And we were flying . . .

You were looking straight into my eyes . . .
Your eyes were big and shiny . . .
Honey-color they were . . .

Then you were rubbing yourself to me deliberately . . .
And I was desiring you strongly . . .
You were rubbing yourself to me . . .
You were rubbing yourself to me . . .
And I was feeling your whole softness . . .

O . . . I was sweating . . . I was in a wet dream . . .

Glendale CA 20070109

Secret Glow

You are pretty and beautiful, or you are not,
I do not know, I do not care which one you are not;
Yet on your face, in your eyes, on your lips
There is a smile that attracts my soul.

It is a glow, a smile, a wink,
It has no relation with pretty or beauty,
It is a spark of magic that allures me,
Relates to my feelings wholeheartedly.

The days, the sidewalks, the seashore
All are fascinating with their cute beauty;
There is the pretty, the beautiful, and the charm,
Yet the glow remains in your endowment alone.

The glow remains only in your sight,
Connected with numerous secrets and gossips,
And the days of our life, the sidewalks and the seashore
Guard closely, properly, faultlessly . . .

But you do not seem to believe me,
My whisper breaks down in silence . . .
Whereas it is the same glow that slightly
Flashes in your sight with love.

While the tale of pretty and the beauty is not a legend . . .
I wonder . . .
Do you know? Do I not know? How then . . .
I seem to be grasping the secret of the glow . . .

Glendale CA 20070109

Inspired

The harp of my life is resounding now with fascination,
Granting delights to my heart and soul;
The ominous tune of sadness, pain, and longing is no more,
That used to cut my breath short whenever remembering the past.

It is a mild, blonde autumn; the sun is a handful of gold
Scattered on my path, that takes me to the home of my hopes;
My car is cruising fast, without feeling
That has grown older, together with me, yet remaining the same crazy.

I will soon arrive at the garage of my old house,
I will announce my arrival by ear piercing honk;
I will read the word of satisfaction on the sight of my beloved,
I will have my share of bread and butter with a clear conscience.

Thus, I am taking my exit on the freeway
That takes me to the street close to my heart;
The forthcoming years seem to be delightful
Which inspire me with energy and grant me flying wings.

Glendale CA 20070113

Loss

Light and dark,
Light and dark,
It is dusk;
The night is, is not discernible.

He barely passes the lane,
Turns the bent,
Reaches the dream;
It is so good,
It is so sweet,
His wishes are realized.

Dark and light,
Dark and light,
It is twilight,
The morning is, is not discernible.

Finally, the light increases,
Twilight melts in the light;
The dream disappears.

He stops,
Returns,
Passes the bent,
Seeks the dream.

It is morning,
There is no dream left . . .

Glendale CA 20070119

The Music of Your Name

Your name is sweet music to my ears,
That stirs me, vibrates my heart.
Like a field, I thirst for your purling,
To flower with plentiful colors.

The blushing moon slides up
Imitating your gliding steps
Passing through the web of my love,
Your pretty feet become dewy
And I realize the extent of my love
For you.

It is after so many tears
That love becomes crystallized,
Becomes dews,
Otherwise, it would have rimed,
And you would have chilled in abandoned roads.

It is the fire of love which evaporates the rime
And the dew drops on your way as a smile
Decorate your way with a grand promise,
Joining with your faith and goodness.

I always see stars in your eyes,
Your glance always reflects stars;
Bright rays are beams of light
Reverberating in the horizon.

How is it that you fill my heart with such love?
So, I love you when the day breaks, the night falls;
The morning breaths into me hope,
And the music of your name resounds.

Glendale CA 20080202

Accomplishment

Whenever you look at me
And I feel you are brimming with desire,
The mania hits on the sunny side of my heart,
I become warm
Like a piece of rock,
And I shine with smoothness,
I shine.

Whenever you put your hand on my chest,
Your palm fills with my warmth,
By which you become sweeter
Like the ripeness of late autumn.

We feel torrid,
We feel torrid,
And gasp breathlessly.

Do not worry,
This heat will not melt me,
I will sustain enough.

You dispose yourself into my arms
And let my sultry deluge you,
Deluge you.

The ripple flies us
Over the summits of frenzy.

I need to have the power
To cleave all the bonds,
Present you satisfaction and peace.

With all our human imperfections
It is with love
That we achieve the perfection of creation,
Totally clean and bare,
With holy devotion,
By which we are discharged,
And recharged,
And become completed with satisfaction,
We become complete.

Glendale CA 20080208

The Most Beautiful Girl

I have found the most beautiful girl in the world;
In the sun of her eyes, her clean glance shines,
In the curve of her warm lips, there are no sins of kisses
And she promises me alone her first kiss.

I love the most beautiful girl in the world,
In the depth of her heart the sea of love swings,
In her soul of devotion is her final sacred promise,
I carve her image at the altar of my heart.

I take the most beautiful girl in the world
Through the golden path of my dreams.
The dawn and the future of my and her fiery love
It is arched and knotted together with the colorful rainbow.

I embrace the most beautiful girl in the world
With my deepest love, with my warmest desires,
By which my world lives, and my hopes are unending,
And the pigeon of my fortune hovers in the bright sky.

Glendale CA 20080217

Dedication of Wine

My heart as a chalice of love, my love as red wine in it,
I am raising my full glass to you, my home people.

With the cherished sacred traditions of Navasard
I drink to your life with fiery good wishes.

Whenever any destructive clouds clashed with you
You endured like the giant of Sassoon of lightning saber,
You stretched out your mighty hand with a heroic victory
And firmly snatched the sun from the midst of darkness.

And you shall nail the sun on the summit of Ararat,
Your own fiery sun is full of the new spirit of new life.

My heart like an incombustible burning raspberry bush,
My love as an inextinguishable flame on its branch,
I drink to your sacred life, my people, my nation.

Glendale CA 20081026

Good Tidings

I will appear in your thoughts with my songs
Dedicated to our love
By which I placed a ring on your finger with a promise,
With a flower of the rainbow on your forehead.

Even if I am beyond the seas
I will leave my heart with you;
Even if there be storm and lightning,
I will come to your bosom
Over the mountains and through the ravines.

Clouds are gathered, my dream is confused,
I cannot see the bottom of the abyss,
Yet in my high endeavors is my purpose,
My path takes me to the summit.

The digger dug a pitfall in his base depths
And himself is at the bottom of the pit,
The moon of our fortune sweeps through the sky
It will not fall in the pitfall.

Stars are shining, and the moon is bright,
The story of my dream is clearing up,
In the blue azure my hopes are afloat
Giving us good tidings of life.

Glendale CA 20090420

Starlit

When did your golden teen pass,
And you became such youthful noble,
With reliable dreams and aspirations
To dedicate songs of my wishes to you.

To expand the clear blue of my love
To become the starlit sky of my belief,
To spread my wishes among the stars
Realizing them with good fortune.

It is a sunny grace of providence
Satiated with your sight and spirit,
Which is colorful with impeccable beauty.
And has been blessed by God reigning in my heart.

Do feel the seething of the family blood
That I have endowed you with secret inheritance,
There is life and secret light of goodness in your days,
Do enjoy and take delight with purpose and unshakeable will.

And do lit up your own light of new life
And add your own star to the sky,
Keep the glitter of my star in your star
And pass it on to your starlit son.

Glendale CA 20090420

Intimate Conversation

Since I have observed you often in silence
And have been in communion with your heart in silence,
You think I have lived an easy life,
And have not associated with anxiety and sorrow.

Yet, often, when I have held your hand
Pulling you as if by compulsion into my arms,
I have wished not to wear out your patience,
An aching heart cannot be cured by reminding the pain.

Yet, often, when I have said: Do not ask, as it will be fine.
And I have not had the patience to elaborate,
I have wished to encourage you in your endeavors
To earn back my losses.

I will lit up the new starlets of your heart
To glitter with the sense of your satisfaction,
In order to eliminate the sorrows of both of us
The way the moon scatters the darkness.

Glendale CA 20090422

Nightmarish

For the millions of Armenian Martyrs of
The Armenian Genocide of 1915–1924,
Committed by Turks of the Ottoman Empire & the Republic of Turkey.
A dialog with the Turks.

The torrential wave of blood pounds my chest,
Stirring furiously from the depths of desert,
Rising from dry sand, the slashed breast of my holy mother,
Wherefrom my orphan brother received his dreadful sustenance.

Sustenance from, the slashed breast of my mother . . .
Raped and ravished . . .
Instead of vivifying milk of love
He suckled bitter drops of coagulated and suppurated sacred blood,
The curse of an atrocious world for the mankind.

My orphaned and wretched brother satiated with vengeance,
Who otherwise would have incensed like a censer,
His pure eyes, luminous and compassionate of old,
Were filled with the poison of rancor, perfidious, depressed and dark.

Alas, my loves of spring . . .
Alas, my desires for life . . .
How should I embrace you with docile and sweet enjoyment yet again?
Whereas my brother, who is myself, has identified with my horrid revenge
Suckled from the slashed breast of my holy mother . . .

Love

I knew
That you are like fire,
That should not be touched,
That you will burn.

But my desire was much,
And my love was much.

So, I touched.

Do you see
How beautifully I am burning?

Glendale CA 20150415

Desire

I want to sit in the sun
And count the stars of your eyes.

I want to pluck petals of the flowers
And discover the colors of your eyes.

I want to perch in the garden
And breathe the roses of your eyes.

I want to wander on the seaside
And gather the pebbles of your eyes.

I want to sunbed in the sun
And get warm by the sun of your eyes.

And drink the blazing taste of your lips,
I want . . .

Glendale, CA 20150416

Clean Page

There are some pasts, that
Do not return
Even in memories.

Maybe you are one of those.

Like a black spot.

I am content in my heart,
That like a black spot
You do not appear
On the white pages of my memory.

Glendale CA 20150416

Hope and Glimmer

Do not deprive yourself of hope,
And do not deprive him of hope.
Maybe that is
Your and his only possession,
Hang from just a ray
In your and his heart.

Hope is just a ray,
That has entered my heart.

There is no heart without a glimmer of hope.

Without such vibrant ray
People will turn dark;
And although the universe will not darken,
But will lose a ray.

The fear of obliteration
Germinates from hopelessness,
Begets hate and anger,
Sterile and destructive . . .

Indulge yourself in a day of peace,
Do not make your supreme decisions
In the nightmare of
Hopelessness, or
Lightlessness.

Here hope will twinkle,
The little star of your fortune will flicker,
And in the light of peace
You will formulate your wishes
And your devotion.

The bluebird will hover
And flutter in the dimension of your heart,
And the sun,
It will peck iridescent rays,
It will perch on a beam of light,
Which is reflected from future.

With a trendy intuition
Rise and view yourself,
Notice the buds
Blooming as roses
In a complete flourishing,
Correlating colorfully with your heart,
Your hope and your light,
That might be your and his only possession.

Glendale CA 20151107

Roses Perfume

The breeze of my feelings
Touches me,
Perfumes.

The wave of my wishes
Collides with me,
Perfumes.

Was that not that they used to
Wash the feet of the arriving traveler
And anoint his head with oil;
That washed and anointed Jesus
To relax and rest,
And perfume.

Tranquility perfumes with peace,
Which is the merit of blessed life,
Sparkling in the eyes of children.

At the end of a good day
The sunset is varnished
With colors.

The brimless purple descends
As a royal pleasure,
And erases
The dividing line between heaven and earth,
Covers the horizon with impossible bliss of wishes,
Which is the infinite flowerbed of life.
It perfumes.

The roses of the aromatic garden of life
Perfume.

Approach me with a caress
And endow me your sweetness
To fill my gratification with your perfume.

Glendale CA 20150716

. . . In Order to Kiss

The shadows of my sadness have crowded up
Like the slow-moving bevies of autumn;
The falling leaves swamp my heart
With dry bitterness.

I am grieved like a sacrificial lamb
That is being fed with the last pinch of salt.

The thirst is a pain on my lips,
The frequency of mirages
Darken my vision.
Regrets of the past accumulate
With anxiety and alarm . . .

Where are you,
Termination of my quests,
Adorn my forehead with colorful decorations,
Caress my torments
With the softness of your endearments,
Approach me, approach me,
And present your lips
To my kiss of satisfaction.

Glendale CA 20150718

Singing Angel

The beautiful angel is singing
With the other two,
The song of
Life and happiness,
Joy and pleasure.

She is beautiful
With the gleam of her eyes,
With the sweet of her kissable lips,
Scenting with the red of
Rose petals . . .

Bright as the colors of the rainbow
Adorned with fortune
Life is emanating from
The heart of the beautiful angel
As balm and manna.

Stars are sparkling
In the ponds of her eyes;
Her lips are opening
Like rosebuds.

The beautiful angel is singing . . .

Glendale CA 20150811

The Easiest

She was testing my shyness.
She asked:
"What would you do
If I appear suddenly naked
In front of you"?

I said:
"I will shut my eyes
So that
You would not feel
Ashamed".

She liked it so much
That undressed.

It had never happened
So easy.

Glendale CA 20150530

You Are Beautiful

I love you,
I am effusive with my feelings,
Which are shining on my heart.

With warmth
And love
You are crushing my feelings,
Sparks are spilling out of them,
Everywhere.

It is from them
That stars come into existence.

The sky is full of stars now.

The sky freckled with stars
Is more beautiful than before.

But you are more beautiful,
With the star pair of your eyes,
Which shine more like the sun.

You are more beautiful,
Even from before that, too.

Glendale CA 20180806

Apple of Transgression

You are a sparkling dream,
Appeared in my life
Created a celebration
Yet you are not in the circus.

That is a pretty comedy,
A clever eyewash,
With salty deep,
Deprived of fascination.

You are an exquisite butterfly,
With golden, delicate wings,
As a glitter of the sunbeam,
Enchanting flirtation.

Your lips are as cherry and apricot,
As apple of transgression,
Your bosom is a paradise of love,
The tranquility of cohabitation.

You will not . . . you will not endure
When I touch you with desire
You will melt like a candle
Fallen in the fire.

Come . . . with all your elegance,
Elegant airs and graces,
With your full flavorsome ripeness,
And with the fire of your desires.

I will take you to the blue,
In the colors of the rainbow
I will decorate your way,
I will squeeze the pomegranate of your love.

You will reach to pure intoxication,
The torpor of inebriation,
With my viral magic
In the depth of Milky Way.

Glendale CA 20181209

Your Magic

It is only you
With your touch of magic
Which makes me tremble
When you are on my laps,
And my clasps.

It is only you
And your magic.

Glendale CA 20181213

Dream

Clear and temperamental night,
Lunar light crashes all around,
Grant me to embrace her
In my arms,
And feel her heartbeat,
Her tenderness and devotion.

The soft breeze of her breath
Touches my temples,
And in the silence of the moment
I squeeze the cherries of her lips.

Let her eyes blink through fancy dreams,
Let me steal my delight from her bosom,
With fervent desire,
Warming my heart.

In life
Every creature
Has his share of luck?

That fairness is gorgeous,
Decorated with lush and plush.

Clear and temperamental night,
Feast over the moon
And sparkling stars.

Glendale CA 20181217

Moonshine

There was you,
There was the night,
And there was me.

There was no whisper,
It was your breath,
Which was a murmur.

There was a star,
May be a meteor,
It was your eyes
Which were shining
By the sparks of your desires.

You were hot,
You were scorching,
Putting on fire.

Your tears were soft,
Caressing,
Beautiful,
Honey taste.

In the moonshine
The tale was whispering
A secret story
In the melody of your murmur.

I desire
The moon
Be your eyebrows.

I was getting dark in the night,
I was flushing,
Flirting.

There was you,
There was me,
And the full moon.

I was sleepwalking,
I had become you.

Glendale CA 20190115

Quake

How does the flower feel
When a dewdrop drips
In the heart of the flower cup
In the lovely bed of twilight . . .

It probably quivers
With a love felt feverish fever . . .

That is how I feel
When I (embrace) you by my glance . . .

Glendale CA 20190517

Storm and Hurricane

Your midsummer maturity is more fragrant
Than the spring bloom.

A variety of colors expand in your eyes.

Your bosom has the heat of summer
With the abundance of thy pomegranates,
And red wine drips from the ripe grapes of your lips.

In the deep horizon of your eyebrows
Your glance is fascinating.

Butterflies in my heart are swarming with emotion,
Fluttering with frenzy to drink your aroma.

Craving to reach, to attain the sanctity of your embrace
And to open the veil of my prayer.

My blood-storm is seeking the hurricane of your bosom,
With a longing to ferment and fuse.

Glendale CA 20191223

Your Sweeties

I want you to come and bring
Your fragrances
That fill my pitcher
With the taste of your lips;
That scorch my temples
With the caresses of your gasp;
That whisper endearment
And grant feelings to my thoughts.

I want you to come and bring
Your softness,
That awards me the pleasure
Of your hips and bosom,
And wraps around me
Your thighs,
Exhausts my boil, fever and panting.

Come and bring your soft
And warm effeminacy,
Deep cuddles,
Your favorite sweeties I desire.

Glendale CA 20040324

www.ingramcontent.com/pod-product-compliance
Lightning Source LLC
Chambersburg PA
CBHW071746040426
42446CB00012B/2483